TAKE THE LEAD FOR THE PERFECT RECALL

The proactive approach to lead and recall training.

Tim Jackson

Published by WriterMotive
www.writermotive.com

Contents

Introduction..9

Chapter One Why your walks are such a stress 13

Chapter Two Equipment.. 16

Chapter Three Nothing in life is free 21

Chapter Four The 'Name' Game 29

Chapter Five The Tail Wagging Game... 32

Chapter Six Look at me 36

Chapter Seven Starting your walk off on a calm........................ 43

Chapter Eight Introducing a whistle.. 47

Chapter Nine The Traffic Light System....................................... 51

Chapter Ten The Wobble Game... 54

Chapter Eleven The Middle Command 56

Chapter Twelve Taking your walks outside................................. 59

Chapter Thirteen Letting your dog off the lead for the first time 63

Chapter Fourteen Making every walk into an adventure............. 67

Chapter Fifteen Retractable leads 72

Chapter Sixteen Your key to success... 74

Bonuses 76

About the Author 78

Other Books by the Author.. 80

Acknowledgements 81

<u>Praise for Our Training and Behaviour Programmes</u>

What Some of Our Clients Have to Say About Our Training and Behaviour Programmes

"Our three-year-old west highland terrier wasn't responding well to our new shih tzu puppy. We'd expected jealousy etc., but he was really fearful and became aggressive, withdrawn and generally seemed depressed. He'd stopped playing with us, and we were getting to the point of returning our puppy.

Tim came out and spent some time with us and our westie… of course, it was us that got the training lol! Tim was brilliant, gave an honest assessment of our situation and changes we could make immediately as well as training exercises we could do with the dogs.

After perseverance and practice, we now have two happy dogs and the confidence to continue with the work. I can definitely recommend Tim. Thanks so much for a happier life ."

Vicki Kenyon

"I have a one-year-old Red Cocker and was having a lot of problems with his behaviour – my fault as I totally spoilt him from day one. Tim was recommended by my dog groomer. I rang and booked a telephone consultation. I felt at ease as soon as I spoke to him. He was so lovely and made me feel positive from the start.

We got out of the programme everything we needed. It's up to us now to keep putting in the work we learnt.

After the first lesson, we saw a huge improvement in our dog's behaviour.

I would definitely recommend Tim and Pets2impress."

Sara White

"We bought two puppies and found it extremely difficult to do anything with them; we needed help.

We got with Tim at Pets2impress, who came and did an assessment. He informed us that they had fear-based aggression towards other dogs, and he put our minds at ease, knowing that there was something we could do to help them.

Without Tim's help, I could not have coped. I can't recommend Pets2impress enough ."

Mr and Mrs Selby

"My partner and I adopted a dog from Europe. All was well until three months later when he started to show signs of aggression towards other dogs and men. We contacted Tim for an assessment and booked him for training. We did everything Tim suggested, and now our dog can be around other dogs (even daycare) and people. We now have learnt the tools and techniques needed to recognise when our dog is in a situation he is not comfortable with and we are able to use the training commands to get him out of it which means no more aggression! Thank you, Tim."

Mr S Scott

"I have a male dog called Storm, who is a Newfoundland cross bullmastiff and has an anxiety issue. He got to the point where he is very fearful of strangers and would growl and bark to scare them off. After several weeks training with Tim and him bringing various people along to the house, Storm has now started to relax and is nowhere near as bad as he was. I will continue to use Pets2impress with Storm as I can't believe the results they are having with Storm. I am over the moon, and I can now actually start to relax. If you're thinking of using these guys, then it's money well spent."

Lee Brown

"I have absolutely loved taking part in the online course. I love my time spent with Paddy teaching him new tricks etc., and this course has opened up a whole new load of ideas that I can use and implement on our day-to-day activity that didn't even cross my mind. I thought it was going to be a real struggle for him during this isolation period with the lack of exercise and stimulation that he is used to on a daily basis. He is used to a good 2/3 walks per day as well as 2 – 3 full days at Pets2impress daycare, so naturally, I thought he would be bored during lockdown and bouncing off the walls with energy. During this course, his tail has never stopped wagging, and I've found that he is just as tired at night during this time as he was after a busy day on the go. Thank you, Tim, for everything you have done."

Samantha Heley

"Having the resources from Tim at Pets2impress available through the lockdown has been invaluable. The changes and help provided have kept our puppy active, stimulated and happy! In a massive change to normal routine, my worry was that Cobie would suffer and lose her confidence that she had gained, but instead, she has learnt so much, and we have the knowledge to keep things going after this is over."

Amy McFaulds

"My Black Labrador Charlie had an amazing time completing the online challenges in the Pets2impress 14-day challenge, he learnt a lot, and so did I. It was both fun and educational! I ordered him the isolation pack so he could get some toys and treats as a reward for his hard work. The pack gave me some more ideas on how to challenge him and train him too."
Anni Jowett

" I would just like to say that Tim came to Stockton on tees yesterday to see my Mam with her dog, Mavis, Tim has made my Mam feel that she can help Mavis and my Mam isn't upset anymore now she knows what she needs to do to help her I'm so thankful for your help highly recommend this company thank you so so much. "
Victoria Ainsley

"Thank you so much for all the advice and tips we definitely have a better-behaved pooch but still some training to be continued.
To think just over a month ago, Dave and I were tearing our hair out with a pup who ruled the roost and life was not enjoyable for any of us including Lara.
You have changed our lives, and since being introduced to you, at a web seminar by Katie (dogwood), the combination of training with yourself and scentventure with dogwood we have a relaxed puppy who is so happy, and we are all enjoying being a family!
I honestly can't thank you enough, and I have already spread the word of Pets2impress to a couple of friends who are thinking of getting a dog.
We will continue our training and advice and keep you updated! Thank you again from all of us, we are finally a family!"
Charlotte and Dave

"Thanks for all your help during lockdown. Training Maverick is a work in progress, we are learning a lot along with Maverick. All your ideas and techniques have been very useful, and we will continue to use them. Life during lockdown with Maverick has been a lot easier, we've had fun, and I think you have saved us a lot of stress. We are happy to recommend you."
Tracie and Stephen Cook

"Excellent service. Trainer very knowledgeable and explained everything very clearly and showed us how to do training. Very fun sessions with very happy puppies and owners. Very highly recommended"
Cheryl Murray

"We have been using Pets2impress since its inception. Tim taught our boys to walk on a lead, recall and how to behave as family pets. They've stayed with Tim when we have gone on holiday and loved it. They are walked during the day by Shannon, and I cannot recommend their services enough. Very flexible if you have to make a last-minute change and always happy to help if they can. You've tried the rest... now try the best"

Lesley Elliot – Burn

Introduction

Let us be honest we have all seen dogs taking their owners for a walk or seen owners screaming and shouting at their dog as it refuses to come back to them.

Why do some many owners struggle? Why do so many owners find taking their dog for a walk stressful? Taking your dog out for a walk should be a fun and enjoyable experience for both dog and owner but let's be honest there is nothing more frustrating than a dog that practically pulls your arms out its socket or a dog that would choose to run up to everyone and everything else in the park as opposed to coming back to you.

I am very grateful that my dogs have always had a very reliable recall; however, my previous dog, Lady, was an absolute nightmare on the lead, she pulled me here, there and everywhere.

When she was a puppy, I took the lazy option, I put her in the car and drove her to a big open space, let her out and let her go. I spent most of her walk throwing her ball to try and burn as much energy from her as possible, I'll explain later in this book why that was not the best thing to do.

I knew how powerful she was, so in my head, it was easier doing it this way. As time went on and I started to work longer hours I had to employ a dog walker and guess what, they struggled massively with walking her. She was a 35kg German Shephard and boy did she have some strength, and when she wanted to pull, she pulled.

The dog walker was constantly on the phone explaining how bad she was on the lead, how she had pulled them over and there was one time, she had pulled that hard she snapped her lead.

Not ideal which is why I knew I had to do something with her, I needed to work, and if I wanted to continue working the hours needed, I had to be able to rely on a dog walker, and I didn't want the dog walker to find walking Lady a stress.

One weekend I visited the local pet shop and decided to try a harness, that worked for a couple of weeks, but then it seemed like she was pulling more so I then went back to the pet shop and invested in a head halti which seemed to do the trick, but Lady hated it.

After using it for a few days, I noticed the fur underneath her eyes was gone, and she was left with two red sore areas where the head halti had rubbed so much. This was then causing her further upset when back at home as she was forever rubbing her head on the carpet.

After trying numerous different restraining aids, I knew I had to do something to correct this, and that's when I stopped being lazy and put in the work with her.

I should point out at this time I was a young extremely handsome (if I do say so myself) Auxiliary Veterinary Nurse pretty fresh out of nappies so I did not have a lot of experience with dogs at this stage and I certainly had very limited experience with German Shepherd dogs... you can find out more about the struggles I faced with her in one of my other books, Help! My dog doesn't like being left alone. At this stage in my life, you can have fit my dog training knowledge on a stamp... it was very minimal.

I spent a lot of time with Lady, and sure enough, by the end, she walked like a dream. In fact, most days I wouldn't have even known I had a 35kg German Shepherd attached to the end of the lead as she would always walk nicely alongside me.

Why didn't I train her to walk nicely on her lead earlier I thought? Why did I spend so much money on different leads, head haltis, harnesses etc.?

Lesson well and truly learnt, if you want a dog to walk nicely alongside you then you need to train them to do so, and you have to remember it doesn't just happen overnight.

As humans, I would say one thing we lack is patience and that's one thing you really need when it comes to lead and recall training and I guess we also need to remember things don't happen overnight, if you want results you have to work for them. I recently signed up to a karate class with my son as we both love the Karate Kid movies and the new

Cobra Kai series, but I never went into the class thinking I would immediately get my black belt. I knew I was going to have to put in the work and be patient. In December 2020 both Harvey and myself gained our yellow belt. A very proud moment for me as I watched my son be awarded with his certificate and belt. Our hard work paid off, we attended classes, during the lockdowns we participated in the zoom lessons and outside of class, we practised every day. We made it fun too, and that's what you should be doing with your dog's training, and that is certainly something I'm going to be sharing with you throughout this book.

I was lazy and inexperienced, but it was thanks to Lady and her 'issues' shall we say that helped me discover my love and passion for canine behaviour and it was thanks to Lady that I trained to become a qualified canine behaviourist.

Throughout this book, I am going to share with you some of my top secrets to help you have the perfect recall and to help you have a dog that walks nicely alongside you.

Do not take the lazy option like I did, put in the work and trust me, you will get the results that no doubt during this moment of time seem like a distant dream.

Dog's need daily exercise, that's a given. However, so many dogs lack daily exercise because owners find walking them so frustrating and stressful, and they find it easier to have a game of ball in the garden. Trust me when I say it doesn't matter how big your garden is, your dog needs to get outside of the house and explore and most importantly make use of his natural senses.

In 2020 we were faced with one of the worst medical emergencies seen in the last 100 years, and as a result, the country had to go into a full lockdown. I, for one, did not cope well with being stuck at home and only able to go out for 1 bit of exercise each day. I am naturally an outdoors person, and I enjoy being outdoors and exploring new places.

I know I was not the only person that struggled in the country, it was tough for everyone, but the point I am trying to make is we appreciated how boring it was being stuck indoors for pretty much 23 hours per day but yet so many people find it perfectly acceptable to leave their dogs stuck indoors for days on end. It is no wonder that when they do finally get out, they are full of energy and choose not to listen to a word you are saying.

When restrictions were lifted for the 2020 lockdown, I was bursting to be outdoors and brace some of the glorious weather we had as well as get back to work and get back into some form of routine.

To some, it is easier to have their dog remain indoors and give them a few games of ball in the garden, but I know that's not you, otherwise, why would you be reading this book?

I am going to help you achieve a perfect recall and have your dog walk alongside you on a loose lead, but it is important to point out now that I do not believe in choke chains, spray collars, shock collars or any form of negative based methods of training, so if that is what you are looking for, I suggest you look elsewhere. I learnt the hard way that negative based methods of training never correct the problem, and I want to help you correct the problem, not just hide it away and pretend like it is not there.

There is no point in reading this book and then putting it on the shelf and thinking 'oh I enjoyed that'. You need to put in the work and understand any form of training can take time and always requires a lot of patience.

Once you have read this book, you will know some of my top secrets to have that perfect lead and recall training.

Before we look at some of my top tips, we need to understand why dogs appear to make walk times so difficult… believe it or not, it is not actually their fault.

Chapter One
Why your walks are such a stress

When you first welcome your dog into your family, I am sure you imagine that walks will be a fun and enjoyable experience for you and your dog, but reality quickly kicks in and before you know it, your screaming and shouting for your dog, or literally getting your arm pulled out of its socket.

So many owners dread taking their dog for a walk because they find the whole experience one huge embarrassment.

Let us start by having a look at why your dog pulls you so much on the lead. If you want to correct a behaviour, you firstly need to understand why the dog is displaying this behaviour.

One of the most common reasons your dog pulls you is because they learn from a very early age, that's how they get to move forward. Every time they pull you take a step behind them and bingo you give your dog a clear signal that pulling actually works so guess what happens... they continue to pull.

Outside in the big open world, there are so many distractions which include other dogs, people, birds, traffic, leaves blowing on the ground, smells and exciting things to see. Most dogs sadly do not get enough exercise, so when they do get that lead on it's the best part of their day.

They pull, to get round the corner or to get to that exciting place you always take them too. At that exciting place, they get to meet new friends or have a play with their ball or just have a jolly old run around.

You know that feeling you had when you were a kid on Christmas morning, and all you want to do is race downstairs to see if Santa has been? That level of excitement is what dogs feel when they are out on their walks.

When you take your dog for a walk, let us be honest we see so many owners being walked by their dog and something I see every walk I go on with my dog is other owners constantly pulling back on the lead or keeping the dog close to them on a tight lead.

By pulling back on the lead, you actually reinforce the dog to want to pull further, it is something called oppositional reflex (do not worry I won't put any more big words like that in this book). This basically means that when your dog is pulled in one direction, their body will lean or even strain in the opposing direction to help maintain balance. So from a human's point of view, I get why owners pull back on the lead as in our head by pulling back we feel this will teach the dog to walk alongside us, but in fact, it actually reinforces the pulling behaviour… I can see you shaking your head thinking "oh man, I do this all of the time with my dog!"… Don't worry, most owners do, but once you have read this book that will all change.

Another issue you see is owners that wrap the dog's lead so tight around their hand to try and keep the dog close to them. This is never a good idea as you teach the dog that a tight lead is what gets them to walk forward and as soon as there is any slack they will invertedly pull once again. Think of it like a pull back car that when you pull back and release, off it goes. The same principles apply to dogs, as soon as they see or feel any slack they are off but not because they are being 'naughty' but because we have taught them to seek tension in the lead.

Finally lets touch upon retractable leads. I get why owners use them; it's a way for the dog to have some freedom whilst still remaining on a lead; however, when they have full stretch of the lead what do they do? They go as far as the lead will stretch and the once again you teach them that by pulling they get to move forward. We will be discussing more on retractable leads later in this book, but I will warn you now, I am not a fan of them.

It is important to understand that dogs do not pull because they are naughty, they pull because that's how they know to move forward, that is what we taught them, intentionally or not.

So now that we understand a little more on why our dogs are pulling, let us have a look at why they choose not to come back to you.

Coming back to you when off-lead is a choice that the dog can choose to make or ignore. We have to remember as with lead training when outdoors there are so many distractions, and dogs learn from a very early age how much fun being off-lead can be. They can play with their mates, chase after squirrels, meet new people and just have fun which is sadly something a lot of dog's lack indoors.

The outside world is a fun place for dogs, and if we are not going to make ourselves fun, then why would your dog make the choice to come back to you?

Throughout this book, I am going to share with you how to make your walks into an adventure, how to keep your dog focused on you, how to make your dogs choose to be with you as opposed to chasing everything else they see and trust me when I say if you follow the tips within this book, no longer will your arms be pulled out of their socket.

I want to show you how to make your walks fun from the second you leave the house to the second you return. I want to show you that throwing a ball constantly on the field is not what your dog needs, and it certainly is not what will help you have the perfect recall.

Teaching your dog to walk alongside you on a loose lead or have that perfect recall takes a great deal of patience and time but trust me by the time you have finished this book you will be dying to go out with your dog, even if it is just to show off to other dog owners how clever your dog is… just remember to send others to this book when they comment on how good your dog is on and off-lead and drop my name into the conversation a few times, naturally only saying good things, of course.

Before we start with the main training lessons, we need to have a look at the equipment we will need moving forward for our dog's lead and recall training.

Chapter Two
Equipment

When it comes to lead and recall training, it is very important that you have the right bit of equipment to help with the job in hand.

No doubt you have invested a lot of money in different restraining aids in the past that haven't done the job and trust me when I say, you do not need to be spending a lot of money on different restraining aids because ultimately, they are not going to correct the issue; instead, they may just mask the issue for a bit.

A number of years ago, I ran a lead training special offer which involved an on-off appointment. I gave 100% money-back guarantee that by the end of that 1-hour appointment I would get that dog walking alongside the owner on a loose lead.

To many that may seem impossible and trust me when I say I am no wizard, I have never attended Hogwarts school of witchcraft, and I don't have a magic wand that I wave over a dog and suddenly they have the ability to walk nicely on a loose lead. However, I do know a number of secrets that will help you get your dog walking on a loose lead.

As you can imagine, the special offer was a huge success as many owners struggle with their dog's lead training and as it goes, I did not have to refund a single person that signed up to the offer, and by the end of each 1-1 lesson, I had that dog walking on a loose lead alongside their owner.

There was this one house I visited with a lovely 5-year-old little dog. When I had the initial phone call with the owner, they informed me that they had tried everything to get that dog to walk alongside them and they were not feeling very confident that I would be much help; however, they did have the 100% guarantee offer so if all failed, they only lost a little bit of time.

When I arrived at their house, they opened up their cupboard, and I kid you not, it was like they had their very own little pet shop. The number of different leads and harnesses and various other restraining aids was unbelievable. They had clearly spent a lot of money in the past trying to correct this issue.

They asked me what I wanted to use, my response was "just his collar and lead will be fine". I think at this moment in time they were just waiting for me to open my cheque book and give them a full refund however after just 15 minutes I had the dog focused on me and after about 30 minutes he was walking nicely alongside me on a loose lead.

I then handed the lead to the owner, and after a few attempts, they too had him walking alongside them on a loose lead. As you can imagine they were blown away and no doubt thinking why did we pay all of this money in the past, why didn't we ring Tim Jackson earlier.

I bumped into them a few months later at a car boot sale, and they informed me how he was still walking lovely alongside them on a loose lead. Five years of trying and five years of investing in different restraining aids all to be told by me that a collar and lead would be all they needed.

The point I am trying to make is you do not need to be spending huge amounts of money when it comes to lead and recall training, and in fact, the things you need are quite minimum. During this chapter I will be discussing the different pieces of equipment you will need to help with your dog's lead and recall training but before that let us just have a look at some restraining aids available and why I would not recommend you get them.

One thing many owners are choosing to use these days are harnesses, they seem to be the go-to piece of equipment, but I personally feel these are a bit of a false economy. When I think of a dog that wears a harness, I automatically think of a husky and what is the job of a working husky... to pull a sledge, and there is that key word... pull! I tried a number of harnesses with my old dog Lady when I was attempting to get to walk nicely on a loose lead, but the issue I had was when she realised, she could put her full weight into the harness and pull harder, she did.

I read reviews on different harness, and I am guilty that I tried a number of different types, but each time resulted in the same thing, she pulled. I didn't need the harness, I needed to put in some lead training with her.

Before I realised that though I also tried head haltis, this certainly helped, however, it was uncomfortable for her, and she didn't enjoy wearing it. People used to mistake it for a muzzle and avoid her, and she ended up with sore patches under her eyes where she had been pulling. She also spent the majority of her walks attempting to pull it off, or she would rub her head on the floor as it was clearly uncomfortable for her. Her walks should have been fun, but at this point, she was more focused on trying to get the halti off her head, and it clearly was not an enjoyable experience for her.

After I spent a number of pounds on different things, it was time to not look for a quick fix but instead invest in the time to train her to walk nicely, and that's just what I did. It was time to scrap the harnesses and head haltis, and instead, I went for a collar lead.

Before I move on, I would like to stress if you have a brachiocephalic breed i.e. pugs, Shih Tzu, Boxer, basically anything with a flat face then a harness would probably be the better option and that's not me contradicting myself, but a harness will put less pressure on their trachea and not cause further issues to their breathing. If you do need to go down a harness route because you have a flat-faced dog, then I would advise a Y fronted harness as these will not affect your dog's joints or natural gait as most other harnesses do.

Most restraining aids are classed as negative based methods of training, and I personally am all about getting a dog to do something because they want to not because they are forced to or because they are scared if they don't then they will experience pain or discomfort. I personally am not a fan of restraining aids, and I learnt the hard way, which is why I hope this book will help you move forward in a positive way with your dog's training.

Let's have a look at certain restraining aids I would not advise

- Choke collars
- Harnesses (unless you have a brachiocephalic breed)
- Head Halti

- Electric shock collars
- Spray collars
- Pet corrector sprays

The above may help, but it will never fully correct the issues you are facing. If say one day you forgot to place the electric shock collar on or you forgot to take the pet corrector spray out with you there is nothing stopping the dog from reverting back to old ways.

What I am going to teach you in this book will get your dog walking on a loose lead and coming back to you because they want to not because they feel forced or scared that if they don't something bad will happen.

Let's have a look at what you will need moving forward

- Collar and Lead

I personally prefer the training leads but, in all fairness, a normal dog lead is all you need, and this does not include retractable leads. With regards to a collar, you want to avoid any form of choke collars including half choke collars. I personally prefer the quick release collars, and as long as you can fit two fingers down either side, then it is not on too tight. So many owners have a very loose collar on their dog and then wonder why the dog slips out of it. Do not forget though, when out in a public space, legally your dog needs to wear a collar and identification tag. An identification tag needs to legally have displayed on it, your surname, the first line of your address and your postcode.

- Whistle

When we move on to recall training, I am going to share my secrets on how you can train your dog to the sound of the whistle. I personally would avoid silent whistles, and I like the acme whistles which you will find a link for on our website, www.pets2impress.com. The good thing about a whistle is it can be heard up to two miles away by your dog which trust me is far further than you screaming and shouting goes.

- Long Line

It can be scary letting your dog off their lead for the first time, and to some, a long line may be what you need to help work on your dog's recall but having the reassurance that you still have control of him. Once you have read this book and implemented all of the lessons, I doubt you will need the long line for very long, but it is a good starting point, especially if you have never let your dog off the lead before.

- Treats

It goes without saying that many dogs will work for food, and if that is your dog, then make sure you are stocked up with some extra yummy high-value treats such as chicken or ham. Remember outdoors there are a lot of distractions you need to have something that your dog is prepared to work for.

- Your dog's favourite toy

Do not just rely on treats, make use of your dog's favourite toy and make sure you have that with you on every walk. I personally find the toys with squeakers are a great way to get your dog's focused back on you.

Believe it or not, apart from poop bags and water, that's really all you need. You may be reading this chapter thinking no way but trust me, you will think differently once you start implementing all of my secrets that I am about to share with you.

Before we can get into the nitty-gritty tips, we need to go right back to the basics and start as we mean to go on by introducing a learn to earn programme and that is just what we will be discussing in the next chapter.

Chapter Three
Nothing in life is free

Dogs love to earn, and they are naturally very attention-seeking little creatures however if dogs do not learn the value or earning things then how can we expect them to walk nicely on a loose lead or how can we expect them to have that perfect recall.

We need to start as we mean to go on, so to begin with, we need to introduce a programme called 'Nothing in life is free', or in other words a learn to earn programme.

One of the nicest things you can do for your dog is to increase their confidence and independence and by implementing a 'Nothing in life is free' programme you will do just that plus you will teach your dog that if he wants something, he has to work for it.

Dogs love to learn, and they love to work, and by encouraging your dog to do that, you automatically increase confidence and independence and set your dog up for success.

Now nothing in life is free doesn't mean we have to send them to work every day or get them to wash the car, pick up the shopping or crack on with the housework. It basically means if the dog wants something, he has to do something in order to get it.

Think of it this way, why do we go to work? Personally, I love work, but for most, it is to get paid at the end of the month. You have to put in that work to get what you want in the end. Or think of a vending machine, the first thing you have to do is put in your money and then once you have done that you get the reward i.e. the sweets or the can of Pepsi.

As of now, your dog should work for everything so for example if he wants his dinner, have him sit or wait first; if he wants to go for a walk, get him to sit or if he wants to play with the new exciting toy you have just bought for him get him to lie down.

Personally, I do not mind what you get him to do, but he should do something in order for him to get something. Think of it like teaching a child to say please and thank you.

Everyone in the household needs to follow the same rules as this programme will not only make your dog more confident and more independent it will help with any aspect of your dog's training.

We also need to put a stop to any attention-seeking behaviours and let me shout this loud and clear... I am not saying you cannot love your dog and I am certainly not saying you should not give your dog attention... what would be the point in having a dog?

We just need to make sure that all attention is invited by us and not the dog so, for example, imagine being sat on the settee on a night time watching television (I can't lie it would be Coronation Street for me!) and the dog comes and plonks one of his toys on you, waiting for you to throw it. This would be classed as attention on his terms; therefore, we should ignore these behaviours. You may find that the dog tries his hardest to get your attention, but it is very important that this is ignored.

There are three very important lessons to remember when it comes to ignoring your dog 1. Do not look, 2. Do not touch and 3. Do not speak – by breaking any of those rules you may as well put him on his back and give him a belly rub just for being cute.

If say after 30 minutes he gives up and starts to walk away, and providing you want to, which I am sure you will, call him to you and give him lots of fuss and attention and by all means spend the rest of the evening playing with him, cuddling him, kissing him... whatever you like to do really.

So, by doing it this way, we can still give the dog attention, but now it is on our terms and not on the dogs.

It is not a case of trying to punish the dog as many would see it, in fact, it is the opposite we are implementing these steps to help build up confidence and independence, and we are teaching the dog, it's ok not to have attention from Mam or Dad every second of every day, I can quite happily entertain myself.

That is the first important change you must make moving forward. Now let us have a look at another very important aspect, a routine.

Dogs are creatures of habit, and they love to predict what is coming next, and we know the importance of a routine, we only need to think of how much our routines were thrown out the window during the COVID-19 Pandemic.

Dogs, like us, respond very well to routine and structure. Naturally, we want to keep things fun and exciting for the dogs too, so I always advise a varied routine, and I will explain what I mean by that now.

A routine for dogs should consist of five things, and these are:

1. Feeding Times

Ideally, our dogs should be fed twice per day and at a similar time each day. Now I don't advise varying the diet, but I would advise varying the way you feed your dog.

Make feeding times fun and make your dog work for his meals. I very rarely use a food bowl for my dog, Buddy, instead I get him to work for his food, so this could involve placing his food in a Kong toy, a scatter feed in the garden, a homemade brain game or a puzzle game you can buy from the shops.

In fact, sometimes, I even use his daily allowance and do a training session with him.

We cannot forget food is a reward; therefore, he needs to work for it (Nothing in life is free) so ask him to 'sit' and 'wait' first before releasing him. By spicing up mealtimes, you encourage your dog to work for his food, and in the process, your dog is getting mentally stimulated, which is a great way to help burn excess energy off your dog, which will ultimately help with your dog's lead and recall training.

One of Buddy's favourite games is to hang his Kong from the washing line. It takes him a long time to get the last bit of kibble, and he is always shattered afterwards… win-win.

As with any form of mental stimulation, every 10 minutes equivalates to a 45 minute on lead walk so by the end of the day, I have a very sleepy and calm dog. In the bonus section of this book, I have included a free handout called recycle the recycling which will give you some great starting points to help spice up mealtimes.

Now we can have a look at the second part of your dog's daily routine.

2. Walk Times

It goes without saying dogs need to be walked every day not just when the weather is fine! Walks are fun for your dog, and they give your dog the chance to make use of their natural senses, i.e. touch, smell, taste, sound and sight.

Walks give your dog a change of scenery, imagine being stuck indoors day in day out with no form of interaction... no doubt you would get bored pretty quickly which naturally would have an impact on your wellbeing, the same applies for dogs, and it is mostly dogs that lack a lot of exercise that develop behaviour or training issues.

Dogs do not have the luxury of popping out when they like. They rely on us as owners to take them out. Walks shouldn't just involve heading to the field to throw a ball you should be making every walk into an adventure – certainly something we do at Pets2impress with the daycare dogs.

Later in this book, I will be discussing how you can make a 1-hour walk feel like a 4 hour walk for your dog.

3. Training Times

In an ideal world, we should be spending 3-4 times per day for 5-10 minutes training our dogs. This is a massive confidence builder and will massively help to reduce anxiety in your dog. Always start the session with something you know your dog can do reliably well and always end the session with something your dog knows as this helps to keep sessions positive.

In between, start to teach your dog new things. Trust me, when it comes to training your dog, you can be as imaginative as you like as longs you and your dog are both having fun, nothing else matters.

Regular training sessions are a great way to reinforce the Nothing in life is free programme, and in fact, it will help encourage your dog to want to work more for things which, that's right you guessed it, will help with your dog's lead and recall training.

During training times, you should also implement some form of brain game such as a puzzle game or scent work as the two work hand in hand together, and both will play a huge part in reducing your dog's energy levels as well as helping to build confidence.

I often advise something I like to call 'recycle the recycling' which basically means if you are about to throw something in the recycle bin STOP and think "can I make this into a brain game for my dog?" The answer is normally yes, and it's so simple to do but has unlimited benefits for your dog.

An example would be a toilet roll tube, cut it up into rings and then interlock those rings together to make a ball shape, post a couple of treats within and then bingo you have a homemade brain game.

Seconds to create but lots of fun for your dog. If he destroys it who cares, it was going in the recycling anyway.

During the Lockdown, I introduced a 14 day online challenge for owners to take part in with their dog. Each day they were given a new challenge which involved either teaching a new trick or creating a brain game. The feedback from this challenge was crazy, one client said

"I have absolutely loved taking part in this group challenge. I love my time spent with Paddy teaching him new tricks etc., and this group has opened up a whole new load of ideas that I can use and implement on our day-to-day activity that didn't even cross my mind. I thought it was going to be a real struggle for him during this isolation period with the lack of exercise and stimulation that he is used to on a daily basis. He is used to getting 2-3 good walks per day as well as 2-3 full days at daycare per week, so naturally, I thought he would be bored and bouncing off the walls with energy. Being part of this group has been great for him, teaching him new tricks and doing things such as jumping over toilet rolls has really helped tire him out both

physically and mentally. His tail has never stopped wagging, and I've found he is just as tired at night during this time as he was after a busy on the go day."

Now bearing in mind at the beginning of the lockdown, we were restricted to one bit of exercise per day. Because the above owner implemented the training, she learned from the online challenges she still had a tired and happy dog by the end of the day… with less exercise than normal.

To really help reduce your dog's anxiety, to build up confidence and independence, I cannot stress how important regular training sessions are with your dog. Do not forget these too should be varied, so do not just focus on the same training sessions each day, trust me, your dog will get bored. This now moves us on to the next part of the routine.

4. Regular Playtime

As with the training sessions, you want to aim for a minimum of 3-4 playtime sessions per day with your dog, each session being around 5-10 minutes long.

Vary the toys that you play with, and don't forget rule number 1, if the dog wants to engage in some playtime with you, then he needs to work for it and why? Because nothing in life is free!

Buddy, as like most dogs, has numerous toys but I only ever leave out 3-4 at any one time. I rotate these toys every couple of days to give him something new to play with and to keep things fun for him.

During our playtime sessions, I bring out one of his special toys. I then ask him to sit, and once he has, we continue with our play session.

This is a part of the day that Buddy adores, his favourite toy being an old crock which now does not really resemble any form of footwear but he loves it, and I make use of this on numerous occasions, believe it or not, it's my go-to item to get him back to me when he is off-lead because when he sees that nothing else matters.

Any form of active play helps keep your dog's heart healthy, keeps the joints lubricated, and improves their overall balance and coordination. Active play sessions also have a huge impact on a dog's mental health, keeping them happy, building confidence and most importantly keeping anxiety levels down.

When choosing toys for your dog always try and aim for ones that encourage your dog to make use of their natural senses for example toys with various textures or toys that can be stuffed with treats such as the Kong range.

Remember, playtime should be fun for you and your dog, and it's a great way once again to build on that strong bond you already have with your dog.

We are now ready to move onto the final part of the routine, a very important aspect of any dog's routine.

5 – Quiet time

If you implement the above (which you should), naturally it will tire your dog out a lot more than he is used to; therefore, it is very important that he is able to rest throughout the day. Dog's should have their own space that they can go to for some chill time. This could be a bed or a crate but somewhere where the dog feels safe and secure.

We know what our moods are like if we don't get a good night's sleep, we can be moody, argumentative, angry, emotional… the list goes on. Dog's too, like us, need their sleep.

Imagine what effect it would have on you if your sleep was disturbed every night? I'm a Father of 3, trust me, I know!

If your sleep pattern keeps getting disturbed, then this will have a huge impact on your mental wellbeing and energy levels. A dog that doesn't get enough downtime can become very stressed and anxious, and it can play a massive part on their day-to-day life and in some cases can lead to aggression as the dog gets frustrated a lot quicker or less tolerant.

Make sure when your dog goes to his bed he is not disturbed, if you have children at home then make sure his sleeping area is away from the children and actively encourage your dog to have a little nap. All three of my children know that if Buddy is in his bed, then he shouldn't be disturbed… I wish Buddy would follow the same rules when we are in bed.

Dogs love to know what is coming next and throughout this chapter, we have discussed the foundations of what you need to implement to ensure your dog gains confidence, independence and burns off energy indoors.

In the next chapter, we start our first main lesson; however, everything you have learnt from this chapter must be implemented first. Use this book as a guide and implement the steps chapter by chapter... trust me, by doing it this way you will get a better and quicker result and hopefully not get overwhelmed by all of the lessons to follow.

Chapter Four
The 'Name' Game

What we need to remember is sadly our dogs do not know their own name. I would love to think that my dog Buddy knows his name and when he meets new friends down at the beach he tells them his name is Buddy, but the sad reality is dog's do not know their name.

They can, of course, build an association to the word, just as they can with the word 'sit' or 'down' but without meaning to burst your bubble, I am afraid to say that your dog does not know they have a name.

They are a different species to us, they think and act differently, and when it comes to training, we have to think dog, especially if we want to get the best results.

As owners, we spend a lot of time focusing on the negative behaviours displayed by our dogs, and we let the good behaviours pass us by. However, by doing that you are actually reinforcing the negative behaviours and encouraging your dog to repeat them time and time again.

Be honest, have you ever sent your dog to their bed for being 'naughty' or have you ever had to give them some time out in another room for 'being naughty'? I'm guilty of this, I did it a lot with my old dog Lady (before I knew any better of course).

No doubt my neighbours were forever hearing me say things such as "Lady, you bad girl, get to your bed" or "Lady, whose done that?" but by doing that I was actually building up a negative association to the word Lady.

We are all guilty of using our dog's name as a negative and eventually, over time the dog starts to associate that particular name as a negative and then we wonder why they won't come back to us when we call their name.

There are so many dogs that I have worked with over the years that do not even recognise their name when you call them, this could be down to a negative association, or it could be down to the fact that the owners have never built up a positive association to their name.

Within this chapter, I am going to explain how you can start by building up a positive association to your dog's name. You will be pleased to know it is really simple however this particular lesson is just as important as any of the other lessons I will share with you so make sure you spend an adequate amount of time working on this lesson before you move on to the next lesson.

Playing the name game

1. You need to begin by having some yummy high-value treats, personally I find chicken or liver work the best with my dog.
2. Start in a quiet area i.e. your living room and whilst your dog is looking at you, say their name.
3. Immediately mark and reward. Make sure your 'good boy' followed by the treat is within 3 seconds of saying your dog's name.
4. Practice makes perfect so make sure you practice this step a few times a day, spending around 1 minute each time.
5. Once you think your dog has associated the sound of their name to something yummy, you now need to say their name when they are looking away from you.
6. Patience may be the key in this particular lesson, especially if you have a greedy Labrador who refuses to break any form of eye contact when he knows you have some yummy goods in your hand. You can try and hide the treats behind your back, avoid any eye contact and look away ever so slightly. Once your dog looks away, say their name and if they turn quickly to look at you mark that behaviour immediately with a yummy treat and a "good boy".
7. Repeat, repeat and then repeat some more. As with the beginning part of this lesson, you want to aim to practice this stage a number of times throughout the day. Remember, every dog is different, and every dog learns at different levels, so be patient and just remember this lesson will take as long as it takes.
8. When you get to a stage where your dog is performing the command correctly, you can then start to add some distractions. You can ask another member of your family to make a noise i.e.

clap their hands, walk out of the room or into a room. When the dog looks at the other person making the distraction, say their name and when they look back at you immediately praise and reward with a yummy treat.

9. Start with minimum distractions to begin with and gradually as your dog is responding more to the command, you can look at increasing the level of distraction. Even taking the training into the garden or the front street will provide lots of different distractions.

This particular lesson should not take a huge amount of time if done correctly, and you should take your time; however, as already mentioned, every dog is different. Just like us, dogs learn at different levels, so be patient, have fun and take your time.

Moving forward, it is really important that you do not use your dog's name as a negative anymore. From now on the name should only be used as a positive and trust me as we move through the lessons within this book by creating a positive association to their name, it will really help you outside in the big open world.

Now that we have your dog's attention, it is now time to move on to one of my next top tips, and that is 'The Tail Wagging Game'.

Chapter Five
The Tail Wagging Game

Now that your dog understands that hearing his name results in good things, it is now time to play a new game, and that game is the tail wagging game.

Believe it or not, it is just as the name suggests, we need to get your dog's tail wagging.

I don't mean just a gentle sway from side to side, I mean a good old helicopter wag, a wag that takes the whole body with it.

No-one knows your dog better than you; no-one knows better than you what your dog loves, and we need to use that to our advantage.

This game is a great game to play with other members of the family, see who can make your dog's tail wag the most, who needs to act the silliest to achieve that full-body wag.

Of course, you will need to experiment but make sure you record your progress, for example, does your dog's tail wag when you bring out his favourite toy? Does your dog's tail wag when you bring out his yummy treats?

This is an important lesson and again one that should not be forgotten about because by finding out what makes your dog's tail wag you can take that outdoors when you are out on walks.

My dog, Buddy, loves it when I play rough with him, he loves it if I jump up and down and he especially loves it when I speak in a high-pitched voice.

Body language plays a huge part in your dog's training, especially when it comes to recall training and there is nothing more fun to a dog that their human jumping around and generally acting the clown. Trust me, your dog will be more inclined to join in and will easily forget about the distractions around him.

How do you think I keep the focus of our daycare dogs on me when I am out on adventures with them? I act the clown and it pays off because they keep their focus on me rather than what is going on around them, another win-win.

Below are some general ideas that you can try at home to see what gets your dog's tail wagging

- Offer treats
- Offer games
- Praise in high-pitched voice
- Rub him lightly and fast along his sides
- Clap
- Move around from side to side
- Roll around on the floor
- Give him his favourite toy.

It really does not matter what you do, you just need to remember the more excitement you generate, the more your dog will focus his attention on you and the more that tail will wag.

Start this game indoors and then once you have discovered what gets your dog's tail wagging the most increase the level of distraction i.e. go out into the gardens and practice some more with the tail wagging game... warning, your neighbours may think you have lost the plot but do not let them put you off, your only priority at this stage is to get that tail to wag.

Keep increasing the level of distraction, you may find as you increase the level of distraction you need to work harder to keep your dog's focus on you, but that is why I advise recording your progress so when you really need to you can bring out the big guns to prevent your dog from running off to the 100 other distractions around you.

One of the main issues a lot of owners have when it comes to recall is, they are generally just boring, and they do not do enough to keep their dog's attention which is why this game is such an important game. This is your secret weapon and once you realise what makes your dog's tail wag the most, what makes him the happiest you can use that outdoors.

One thing I find extremely boring is waiting in a waiting room, especially a doctor's or dental waiting room. There is very little to see (unless you are lucky and they have a fish tank with some fish swimming around) and you just have to wait patiently. At least these days we have our mobile phones to scroll through social media to keep us occupied, I would hate to think how boring it was back in the day when people didn't have mobile phones… technically I am that old; however, I was a child, so I made my own fun back then.

My attention is drawn to my phone because there is nothing exciting going on around me, however, if there was a circus clown, telling bad jokes, juggling and generally just acting the fool as most clowns do where would my attention go? In my opinion, the stupid clown would be more entertaining than scrolling reading people moan on social media.

My focus would then be shifted to the clown because the clown is giving me more entertainment, and that's what you need to do when it comes to the tail wagging game. You need to make sure that all eyes are on you, you need to be the clown.

By being the clown, by beating the distractions, you will get your dog's attention.

The only question left to answer though is… who in your household can be the better clown? Who in your household can make your dog's tail wag the most?

Sometimes you have to experiment with things and remember once again that every dog is different, what motivates one dog may not motivate another. I spend a lot of my mornings going out on adventures with the daycare dogs, and some are motivated by a ball, some are motivated by treats, some just like me acting silly. There are some dogs that are motivated by leaves on the floor or feathers, one dog in particular is very focused on feathers and if I have one in my hand that tail is wagging a plenty and she is not bothered in the slightest with what is going on around her. I can use that feather to my advantage as she will follow it where ever it goes, I can get her weaving in between my legs, running backwards and forwards as she chases it but most importantly, I get to keep her attention on me as the distractions walk on by. Simple, but effective and that's what you need to find… what motivates your dog, what really makes their tail wag and be prepared to think outside of the box.

As with the name game, the tail wagging game is a very big part of your lead and recall training, so make sure you put in plenty of practice before you move on to the next chapter.

When you are ready, we now need to move on to the 'look at me command'

Chapter Six
Look at me

Within this chapter, we are going to attempt to change the way your dog feels when they see another dog or person or in fact, anything that can distract your dog's attention from you so instead of feeling the need to want to pull towards these distractions, jump up, bark etc. we are going to change all of the behaviours to one simple behaviour, and that is getting your dog to look at you in anticipation for a reward.

In order to build up a reliable 'look at me' command, we need to start in an area of little distraction (your home).

We need to devote some time each day to practice stage one of the 'look at me' command (This could be part of your training times, as discussed in chapter three).

The best time to practice is when both you and your dog are relaxed. I want you to get some extra high-value treats, something that your dog would not normally have but something he is really going to want to work for.

Have your dog sit in front of you and wait patiently until he turns his head away from you. As soon as he does, bring the treat to your eyes and say the command 'look at me'. As soon as the dog's head turns and looks at you, praise him immediately (within 2 seconds).

The key to success is repeat, repeat and then repeat some more. I cannot stress enough how important it is that you only use the 'look at me' command indoors to begin with. In order to move on to phase two, we need to make sure we are consistently achieving the results set out in stage one i.e. your dog looks at you every time he hears the 'look at me' command.

Every dog is different just like us, and like us, dogs learn at different levels. Some dogs pick things up very easily, but others can take a little longer. Try not to push your dog too hard and certainly do not get frustrated if they do not do it straight away or as quickly as you would like them to. I always advise not putting a time limit on your training, if it takes a few days great but if it takes a few weeks, that's also fine. When I was at school, it took me pretty much most of secondary school before I could get my head around trigonometry and algebra.

When you feel your dog is performing the 'look at me' command reliably 100% of the time, then you can safely and happily move onto stage two of the training.

Stage two involves upping the level of distraction, which involves practising in the garden or back yard or even the back lane (depending on where you live). In the garden, there are more smells, more noises and ultimately more distractions than you had in stage one.

By now your dog should know the 'look at me' command, and he should know that if he looks at you something yummy is coming his way, if not then you should not have moved onto stage two and I would advise you going back a step and practising some more with stage one.

When in the garden allow your dog to have a sniff around, keep him on the lead so that he does not wander too far as remember to have a reliable 'look at me' command he needs to be close enough so that you can praise him immediately. When having a sniff practice with the 'look at me' command and as soon as he looks give him that yummy treat.

Hopefully, he looked at you but if not never be afraid to go back a step. We want the results, and in order to get those results, we need to take our time and build it up gradually. I would also advise at this stage varying the treats you use (still keeping them of high-value) to help keep it interesting for your dog. You can also use his favourite toy if he responds better to that.

As in stage one, in order to get a reliable 'look at me,' you need to repeat, repeat and then repeat some more. Only when he is looking at you 100% of the time during the training sessions can you then move onto stage three.

As in stage two, we now need to up that level of distraction, and now we are going to practice the 'look at me' on his walks. Stage three is a little bit more difficult because there are a lot more distractions outside in the big open world and what we want to achieve is for your dog to look at you whenever he hears the command. You need to practice in different areas i.e. the street, the park, the beach but starting with quieter areas, to begin with, and gradually building it up. You may find that this stage takes a lot longer than stages one and two, which is fine because remember there is no rush and Rome was not built in a day.

When walking down the street, allow your dog to sniff, look around and every now and then issue the 'look at me' command and keep everything crossed that he looks at you. To guarantee he will, try adjusting the tone of your voice so that it sounds fun and enthusiastic rather than military-style... I would not look at someone if they were shouting or screaming at me.

Again, I want you to keep varying the treats to keep him interested and focused. Over time slowly start to increase the level of distraction when outside so that we can eventually (remember no time limit) reach stage four.

Stage four is where we start to introduce distractions i.e. traffic, people, dogs etc. This stage is perhaps the most crucial, and it is so important that you are patient and focus on your timing.

So where do you need to start?

You need to find somewhere that you and your dog can stand where you can see something that would normally distract your dog, but that place should be a place where your dog is NOT overly bothered about the distractions around him. This could be a big field, it could be the beach, or it could be ten blocks away. It doesn't matter how far away you are initially as long as your dog can see the distraction. This is where your hard work will pay off with the previous training you have been doing with the 'look at me' command.

Once you find a place where your dog is calm and non-reacting, you now need to wait until he looks at the distraction. As soon as he does, you need to issue the 'look at me' command and keeping those fingers and toes crossed, hoping that he looks at you. As soon as he does give him his reward and lots of praise. Remember this is so impressive that your dog has been able to control himself this way, so he deserves the best of treats as well as a good pat on the back.

Every time he looks at the distraction, you need to issue the command 'look at me' and then give him a treat. If he looks at that distraction in the distance 100 times then theoretically, he should have been issued 100 treats. This is why it is so important that you take a lot of treats out with you initially. Do not be tight when it comes to treats and expect to give him a lot in the beginning stages, just make sure you reduce his daily allowance of food to compensate for these extra goodies.

Now I don't want to be responsible for your dog getting the shits and making a mess all over the house so I would advise varying the high-value food to avoid upset stomachs and stay clear of dairy products. I find chicken or liver works really well, or if you check out the bonus section of this book, you will find a link for some homemade dog treats.

As with previous stages, the key to success is repetition. I know you will be edging to move forward but only move forward when you feel you are ready and ultimately when you feel your dog is ready.

We are aiming to change your dog's behaviour around other distractions, and that takes time, lots of patience and consistency so, for example, make sure you watch your dog at all times and be sure to issue the 'look at me' command the second his head turns towards a distraction that would normally excite him such as another dog or a person.

Over time the aim is to slowly reduce the distance between you and that distraction but remember no one gets a medal for being the fastest in this form of training. Slow and steady always wins the race!

If say you began by being 100 metres away from a distraction and you feel your dog has responded well and you decide to half that distance and all of a sudden your dog starts to react problematically do not throw the towel in. Accept that things do not happen overnight, and never be afraid to go back a step because at the end of the day we need to make sure that our dog is ready to progress on to the next stage.

Now in days, weeks or even months you will slowly be able to decrease that distance. I think it is important to point out I do not expect you to take a tape measure out on your walks with you, just use your own judgment.

Take the Lead for the Perfect Recall

The purpose of this particular lesson is to get your dog's focus back on to you. From a dog's point of view, there is nothing more exciting that a play session with another dog but we need to beat that excitement, and we need to know that we can safely walk past a distraction i.e. another dog or a person without your dog attempting to pull your arm out of its socket just so he can say hello.

I am not against dogs socialising, and in fact, I think it is very important for their development that they get the opportunity to play with other dogs however there is nothing more embarrassing than a dog that is dragging you towards another dog or a person so they can say hello.

By using the 'look at me' command correctly, you recondition those unwanted behaviours to one single behaviour, and that is, the dog turning and looking at you when he sees a distraction.

If you allow your dog to run up to everyone and everything he will quickly learn how fun it is to do so and so his behaviour will automatically be reinforced, and he will repeat that behaviour time and time again, making your walks incredibly stressful.

Let us think of a real-life situation

You are walking down the street, and you see another dog heading your way with their owner, from past experience you may be thinking, oh god, here we go again. You may then start to tighten the lead and position yourself in a way where you have a better hold of your dog, but hopefully, if you have taken your time with the previous stages, you can calmly get your dog to walk past any distraction without any concerns.

As you walk towards the other dog and their owner, keep watching your dog and as soon as he looks at the other dog issue the 'look at me' command. Remember the golden rule, every time he looks at the other dog, you need to be ready to get his focus back on you.

I have done numerous 1-1 behaviour appointments with clients, and I find the biggest issue is people's timings and unfortunately this is the most important thing that needs to be spot on in order for this particular lesson to work and get the results that you need. Following that is time, patience and consistency... without them, you will not get the results you want.

Are you fed up of seeing the words time, patience and consistency yet? Don't worry, I will repeat it a lot more as the book goes on.

Dogs are such clever little creatures and pick things up very easily if you reward the behaviour at the correct moment. Just remember treat to repeat, and you won't go wrong.

Eventually and after some training, your dog will start to automatically look up at you whenever they see a distraction. This is something we call the auto watch. The dog at this stage has learnt from positive associations and with repetition that when he sees a distraction if he looks at you, he gets a reward. It is an amazing achievement and one I love to see when helping owners with their problematic pooches. At this point in time you may feel the need to contact me to say thank you so much and by all means, feel free to… or at least me a 5* review on Amazon. In all honesty, you deserve a good pat on the back because you have now successfully achieved what you set out to do at the beginning of this chapter, and you have reconditioned those unwanted behaviours. You have taken control of the situation.

The 'look at me command' has such a number of benefits and in fact, I discuss this particular command a lot in one of my other books, Help! My dog is a devil with other dogs.

It is a great way to regain focus back on to you, it is a great way to re-condition some unwanted behaviours, and it's a great way to prevent those embarrassing moments when you walk past another person or a dog.

I will always recall one day I was walking my old dog Lady in the park near our house, and I saw a man enter the park who was wearing a suit. The man was alone and walked past a lady and her muddy dog.

I am sure you can imagine what happened next, as the man got close to the dog, the dog jumped up and covered the man full of his lovely muddy pawprints. I watched from a distance, as you do and naturally and understandably this man was not very impressed. He could have been on his way to work, he could have had a very important meeting, he could have been on his way to a funeral. The fact is, it doesn't really matter where he was going, I wouldn't have been very impressed either if a dog jumped up at me with his muddy paws whilst wearing my best suit.

The owner of the dog was very apologetic and clearly very embarrassed, so the lesson I want you to take away from this chapter is, don't be that owner. Take control of any situation and know that if you need to get your dog's focus, you can rely on the 'look at me' command in any situation.

Just remember, it won't happen overnight, especially if your dog has spent several months wanting to jump up at people or drag you towards other dogs. These behaviours have been reinforced multiple times in the past we are now attempting to change that, and it sure isn't easy to change a learnt behaviour, but it is certainly not impossible.

This particular chapter is a work in progress and will work much better once you have a dog that walks nicely on a loose lead so let's progress onto one of my next top-secret tips.

Chapter Seven
Starting your walk off on a calm

This chapter is very important because if you want to have a lovely walk, you need to start as you mean to go on. It is natural and understandable why dogs get excited when they see their lead as it means something fun is going to happen but when you have an over-excited dog jumping up at the door, barking and a full wagging body you are immediately setting yourself up to fail.

Throughout this chapter, I am going to show you how you can start your walks off on a calm, so then once you step outside, you have your dog's undivided attention on you.

Dog's learn very quickly what their lead means and they learn through association. As soon as puppies are able to go outside for their walk, most owners are very keen to start their first walk. Over time and through repetition, dogs start to realise that when they see their lead, something good is about to happen.

When Lady was alive, she got very excited when she saw her lead and being a German Shepard, she also became extremely vocal at the thought of going for a walk. She knew it was walk time before I even got her lead from the cupboard, which always amazed me.

Her lead lived in the cupboard under the stairs, and I could go to that cupboard 100 times a day when it was not walk time, and she wouldn't even lift her head, however when it was walk time she knew before I even reached for the door handle.

I found it fascinating that she knew that it was her walk time, and I was interested in finding out what it was I was doing that she associated with going for a walk. Now, I am a man that likes answers; therefore, I decided to experiment with certain things, and I did a number of experiments to try and trick Lady to see if I could get her excited when it wasn't actually her walk time. It sounds a bit mean when I say it like that, but I am the sort of person that likes to find answers or triggers that cause a dog to display certain behaviours, that's my job after all.

43

I went to the cupboard in my dressing gown and picked up her lead, she lifted her head, but she didn't bounce off the walls in excitement. On other occasions, I went to the cupboard in my dog walking clothes but never reached for her lead.

I then tried going at different times of the day to assess Lady's reaction. Maybe I had too much time on my hands, but I was very curious to find out what got her so excited apart from me actually saying the W-word.

The truth is I would have displayed certain triggers that led up to Lady going for a walk, and over time Lady would have associated those actions with the fact she was about to go for a walk.

So during my experiments, because I was not following that particular order of events (the triggers that Lady had gotten used to), Lady did not react. Yes she lifted her head to see what I was doing and to see if I was going to pick up her lead, but chances are she was just showing an interest just in case she missed something else i.e. certain triggers she had seen in the past... make sense?

Now, this didn't happen overnight, Lady would have spent time watching what I did and with the repetition, she soon associated the order of events and the actions I took with the fact it was her walk time. So, for example, before I took Lady for her walk I would always go for my final wee (sorry I know, too much information), I would then come downstairs and put on my shoes and dog walking coat.

I always left out of the back door when I walked Lady, so I would always check the front door was locked, I would then stock my pocket up with treats and poop bags before going to the cupboard for her lead.

We all have our own little rituals and things we do before we leave the house, and there could have been things I did way before going for my final wee that Lady picked up on, something as simple as having a drink (non-alcoholic may I add) or turning the TV off before going for my final wee and because I tend to follow this same routine each time I am going for a walk, Lady soon started to connect the dots and realised walk time was coming.

I needed to know what Lady's triggers were, so I spent some time trying to identify these triggers. I wanted to know at what moment during my leaving routine did she start to get excited or becoming alert knowing a walk was going to follow.

I firstly had to start and change my routine a little bit to desensitise Lady so I would often sit with my shoes and coat on or I would go to the toilet and then come back down and watch TV. The purpose for this was to try and take away that initial excitement before I had even got the lead.

I would also, around 15 minutes before taking her out, do a 10-minute 1-1 session with her to burn some initial energy off her or I would set her off on a brain game whilst I got myself ready. This helped massively as them 10-minute sessions were equivalent to a 45 minute on lead walk so before I had even got out of the house, I had succeeded in burning some energy off her.

Now that was all great; however, she still got over-excited when I reached for her lead so then I had to teach her that this over-excited behaviour she was displaying was going to result in me putting her lead back in the cupboard. I wanted to teach her that when she was calm, that is when she gets her lead on and why? Because nothing in life is free of course. I was rewarding her for displaying calm behaviour.

Every time she attempted to jump up or squeal with excitement, I would put the lead back in the cupboard and go and sit down for a few moments before attempting it again.

At first, she was very confused, and it was difficult to try and ignore a 35kg German Shephard, but I followed the same rules I explained earlier in the book 1. Do not look 2. Do not touch 3. Do not speak.

After several attempts, she was finally calm enough for me to ask her to sit whilst I put her lead on. When we got to the back door, I again asked her to sit and only when she was sitting would I open the back door and let her out and by now you should know why I did that… nothing in life is free. Lady's reward was getting to go out for her walk, but she had to work for it.

By changing my routine ever so slightly, by introducing a short training session or brain game and by promoting 'calm' behaviour I had much more focus and attention from Lady which set my walks off on a positive as opposed to a negative.

Have a look at what trigger points your dog picks up on when its walk time, have a look at introducing a training session or brain game and start promoting this 'calm' behaviour. By doing that you set yourself up for success as opposed to setting yourself up to fail.

If you refer to the bonus section at the end of this book, you will see there is a free gift for you which will give you some examples of how to make your own brain games… don't say I don't give you nothing.

Chapter Eight
Introducing a whistle

When I adopted by dog Buddy, being a sighthound, I knew I had my work cut out for me with regards to his recall training. It is not uncommon for a sighthound to focus their attention on something and boom off they go to investigate, but this was something I wanted to nip in the bud from the very beginning.

Lady was whistle trained, and up until she became deaf, it worked wonders for her, so I decided to train Buddy to the sound of the whistle.

There is nothing more frustrating than a dog that doesn't come back to you when you recall him and because of the job I do I had to make sure Buddy would come when called as how would I ever expect other owners to put their faith in me if I couldn't get my dog back to me.

Before the pandemic and hopefully afterwards at Pets2impress we used to arrange monthly group dog walks which were always the highlight of my month. I enjoyed being out and mixing with different owners and their dogs, and most importantly Buddy always had a blast, but one thing was for sure if Buddy was going to put in a position where he had 50 other dogs to run around with, I still wanted to make he would come back to me when called, and sure enough with the help of my trusted whistle he did just that.

During this chapter, I am going to explain how to introduce a whistle to your dog and how to help build up a positive association.

Which Whistle to Choose?

There are a number of whistles available on the market, but for the past fifteen years I have always recommended an Acme whistle which is available to purchase from most pet shops or if you visit the Pets2impress website, www.pets2impress.com you will find a link for one under the products section.

Whatever whistle you choose, make sure you can hear it when you blow it. I am not a fan of silent whistles and have seen bigger successes from owners that choose a whistle they can hear what they toot.

Where to Start?

Most importantly, you need to begin by having some yummy high valued treats. These treats need to be something your dog doesn't normally have as we want them to associate the sound of the whistle to something extra yummy.

If you refer to the bonus section of this book, you will find a link to download a PDF document which contains a number of useful, easy to make, yummy recipes for your dog...Buddy's favourite has to be the liver cake and apart from the horrendous smell it leaves afterwards it is the one thing he will do anything for, and it only takes a few minutes to prepare.

Think of how excited a young child gets when they hear Santa's sleigh bells ring. They associate them bells with the big man himself and what we aim to do throughout this chapter is to teach your dog that when they hear the sound of the whistle, something yummy is going to follow.

We now need to decide on the way you blow your whistle... behave yourself.

Whether you choose to give a long blow, short blow or multiple toots, you need to decide on your toot from the very beginning and stick to it. If more than one member of the family is going to be using a whistle then between you all, you need to decide on what toot works best for you. Of course, we know that dog's hearing is far more advanced than ours, and they will be able to tell if its Mam or Dad blowing the whistle but where possible we want to keep that toot as close to one another's as we can.

Now it is time to start building up a positive association to the sound of the whistle. If you have ever clicker trained your dog, the same principles apply to building up a positive association with whistle training.

You start indoors where there is little distraction. You have your whistle, your high-value treats, and your dog sat in front of you.

Blow the whistle and immediately give your dog a treat. In an ideal world that would be great if that did the job; however, as with any form of training or positive associations, we need to practice and practice. At this stage of your training, you should not be using the whistle outdoors, it should purely only be used indoors, and in the way I have just described.

You should practice this a few times a day, spending around about 1 minute each session, and all you need to do during these sessions is blow the whistle and issue the treat over and over again.

Very quickly, your dog will start to associate the sound of the whistle to the fact something yummy is going to follow. Spend a few days doing this and then get ready for some games of hide and seek.

Once you feel your dog understands that the sound of the whistle means something yummy is coming, we can now look at building up the level of excitement by playing some games of hide and seek. Now you don't need to be barricading yourself in the loft or hiding in cupboards or under the bed, you simply just need to go into another room, blow the whistle and wait for your dog to find you.

As soon as he does, give him lots of praise and lots of reward. Try to have numerous games of hide and seek throughout the day as not only is it fun for your dog it is also a form of mental stimulating as he uses his senses to locate you.

After a few days of practising, we now need to add in another element of training, and that involves grabbing your dog's collar before treating them.

It may seem strange, but the number of owners I meet that struggle to get their dog back on the lead when they go to grab the dog's collar. The dog learns from association that the movement of the hand towards the collar means playtime is over, so they choose to bounce around and make life very difficult for the owner.

What I aim to do is to desensitise your dog to the collar grab, and we do that at this stage of the training. When in another room, blow your whistle and once your dog comes to you, grab their collar and then issue the treat, praising throughout.

Over time this will become the norm for your dog, they hear the whistle they come, and in order to get the treat you have to grab their collar first. Trust me this will help you out a lot when it comes to recall outdoors which we will be discussing in a later chapter.

To summarise, get yourself a whistle, have some yummy high-value treats and begin by building up a positive association to the sound of the whistle with some yummy treats. Once your dog understands that the sound of the whistle means something yummy is coming, you can then start playing hide and seek around the house. Remember every time your dog comes to you to give lots of praise but before giving the treat, make sure you reach for your dog's collar. This will help with future lessons that will be covered later within this book.

I should imagine at this stage you are bursting to take your training outdoors, but we still have a few more things to work on indoors before we get to that stage so let us move on to the next chapter and start teaching one of my favourite lessons, the traffic light system.

Chapter Nine
The Traffic Light System

This is one of my favourite lessons as it really helps to get your dog focused on you, and it works wonders if you take your time and be patient.

The rules of the game are simple

Red – STOP
Amber – SIT
Green – GO

This lesson should not take too long to master, but it is a great lesson to encourage your dog to walk alongside you. To begin with, you need some high-value treats (no surprises there now), and you need to be in an area of little distraction i.e. indoors.

Place your dog on your right side and hold the treat to your dog's nose. Ask them to **sit** and as soon as the bum is on the floor, reward your dog with that yummy treat. Next, we are ready to **go** so decide upon a command word; personally, I always say 'walk on' and use the treat to encourage the dog to follow and walk alongside you.

The trick is to keep the treat at your dog's nose level (sorry if you have a small dog), initially to encourage them to follow the lure. Say the command word and take one step forward and then praise with that yummy treat.

Initially, we will be focusing on the green, and amber commands i.e the **go** and the **sit** and over time I want you to start withholding the treat on the **go** command and increasing the number of steps you take before giving the treat. The aim is to encourage the dog to walk alongside you and by gradually increasing the number of steps you take before treating the dog you are teaching the dog that being alongside you is a positive as opposed to negative which over time will help reinforce that close command.

When you feel you are at a stage where your dog will walk a good number of steps before you treat, we can now start to take away the lure from the dog's nose. By now, especially if you have taken your time, your dog should understand what is expected of him when you issue the **go** command. Now you can stand up tall (which will be a relief if you have a smaller dog such as a chihuahua) and ask your dog to **go** with the command you have chosen. Walk a few steps and then praise with that yummy treat.

The purpose of this exercise is to teach your dog that by walking forward and alongside you, he is going to get a treat, and it encourages him to remain focused on you.

Now we need to teach the **stop** command, and then we can incorporate all of the commands together to create our traffic light system. As you are walking forward, place a flat palm in front of your dog's face and as you stop issue the **stop** command. As soon as your dog stops moving, give him the treat to reward and mark the behaviour.

As with the go and sit we need to practice with this command as practice makes perfect... or so they say. The purpose of the flat palm is to give your dog a visual, so he starts to recognise the flat palm in front of his head as a signal to stop which will work well as you approach busy roads or distractions in the outside world.

After you have practised, we can now look at incorporating all of the commands together so begin by asking your dog to sit (amber) and then ask your dog to go (green) and after a few steps place that flat palm of your hand in front of your dog's face and ask them to stop (red). Ask your dog to sit and then start the process over again, remembering of course that practice makes perfect.

When you feel your dog has mastered the traffic light system, you can now look at increasing the level of distraction i.e. going into the garden or practising in the back lane. As with any form of training, we start in areas of low distraction and then build up to areas of higher distraction.

Remember the rules, red is stop, amber is sit, and green is go. Begin by focusing on the sit and then adding in the go and finally introducing the stop command.

Once you feel your dog is ready, we can now continue to build up a positive association for the dog being alongside you as we move on to the wobble game.

Chapter Ten
The Wobble Game

Back in the day when I was a much younger Tim, I often enjoyed visiting the local public guest house to have a couple of bevvies with my chums… in other words, I enjoyed a visit to the pub with my mates which often resulted in a very drunk Tim… it only took a couple of pints… I've always been a cheap date, but that's a different story.

Whether you can handle your drink, or in my case, you can't, one of the first signs of being drunk is a lack of bodily coordination that includes the inability to articulate words. A drunk person will stereotypically stumble, fumble, and slur his words. This is due to the presence of alcohol in the blood which affects how the inner ear system works… see I'm not just a pretty face.

Most of us have no doubt wobbled home like a lost penguin after a good night out or in fact seen many others display this wobble walk and it is that wobble walk, I want you to use for this next game. As I write this chapter the date is 31st December 2020 and the North East of England has just been put into Tier 4 which means no one can go out and celebrate the New Year at a pub and instead everyone will remain at home which means by 10 pm I'll be all snuggled up in bed watching a film and will no doubt be fast asleep by the time Big Ben strikes 12.

Although we cannot go out and get drunk, let's just all pretend we are drunk, let us pretend we have just a good night out with our friends and the time has come to go home. Imagine how you would wobble after a good night out.

This game works alongside the traffic light system, and it is another great way to get your dog focused on you and your movements.

Start with your dog on your right side and be sure to be holding some yummy treats. Initially, I want you to use the treat as a lure, and as you walk, I want to you to start wobbling from side to side, imagine the straight-line in front of you wobbles to the left and then to the right and as you follow that wobbly line use the treat to encourage your dog to follow you. Reward your dog after a few steps with a yummy treat to reinforce the dog's behaviour and to help encourage him to stay by your side as you wobble along that wobbly path. Forget the yellow brick road… follow the wobbly road (did anyone else try and sing that in their head or was it just me?)

Over time start to increase the wobbly steps you take before praising your dog and eventually you can then start to add in a command word. I personally would use the command 'close' many would choose the word 'heel'. It honestly doesn't matter which command you use as long as you are consistent and anyone else that gets involved with your dog's training should also be using the same command so that we do not confuse our dog.

Take a few wobbly steps, moving from left to right and with the treat, encourage your dog to walk alongside you. Providing your dog is alongside you issue the 'close' command and then praise immediately with the treat.

Eventually, you want to aim to increase the number of steps you take before issuing the 'close' command, and then eventually you want to stand up tall as you did with the 'go' command from the previous chapter and remove the lure. Make sure you still issue the 'close' command and make sure you still praise your dog for being by your side.

Along with the traffic light system, this is another great game to help build up a positive association of being alongside you. The traffic light system is great to help teach your dog to stop, sit and go, but the wobble game is aimed at reinforcing that close command, and it teaches the dog to want to walk alongside you as opposed of being forced to walk alongside you.

Now we have a list of commands your dog recognises i.e. 'go' 'stop' 'sit' 'close' it is now time to increase the level of distraction and practice them in the garden or back lane.

Before we take the training outside into the open world, we have one more command to work on, and that is the 'middle' command which we will be discussing in the next chapter.

Chapter Eleven
The Middle Command

The middle command is one of the most useful tricks you can teach your dog, and it has a number of benefits. Basically, the middle command is teaching your dog to stand in between your legs.

Once you start teaching the middle command, you will find you use it in a number of situations.

The middle command is a safe place for your dog to be, and it's a great way to help your dog feel connected to you. Think of it like holding hands with a child or a loved one. The middle command, if used correctly, is a real relationship booster.

Examples on when you may use the 'middle' command

- The veterinary practice
- Whilst you wait in a busy waiting room that is potentially filled with other animals and other owners by placing your dog in the middle position you give them a safe place to be, you can keep them focused on you and what is better is you can also feed them easily when in that position.
- Going to the vets can be a stressful experience for our dogs and let us be honest they only go there when they are unwell and when there they get handled by a stranger person, wearing strange clothes and this strange person handles them in ways they are just not used too. It is no wonder so many dogs build up a negative association with the veterinary practice however if you have a reliable 'middle' command you can send your dog to his safe place whilst the vet performs his/her examination, and you can reinforce your dog's calm behaviour by issuing treats. Trust me, it beats chasing them around the consultation room as I did on many occasions when I worked in practice.
- Having a chat with a friend outdoors
- One thing is inevitable being a dog owner, when you are out on a dog walk with your dog, you will at some point bump into someone you know or stop and have a natter with another dog

walker. There is nothing more frustrating than having a dog that lunges you here, there and everywhere as they see other dogs, people walk past etc. By placing your dog in the middle command, you know where your dog is, he is calm, and you can keep reinforcing that calm behaviour with a treat as you have that good old natter with your friend.

- Managing tricky situations
- The middle command is great at helping dogs that are nervous or reactive as it enables you to take away their line of sight of the thing they are nervous of, and it gives them something positive to focus on instead... your pretty face.
- Imagine you are out in the park and you see a flock of pigeons. You know if you don't do something soon your dog is going to turn into an unstoppable pigeon – chasing machine. With the middle command, you can calmly call them to a middle position, spin around to face a different direction and take away the opportunity of your dog seeing it. To your dog, it's a great game, but to you, you have just saved yourself a load of embarrassment.

I personally make the most use of the middle command when it comes to recall. Recall should be fun, which we will be discussing more on how to do that in a later chapter and by having a fun place for your dog to return to it will soon be their favourite place to be plus it is also the perfect position for them to be in for you to put their lead on their collar.

The middle command was something I regrettably never taught Lady; however, it was one of the first things I taught Buddy, and now he loves being between my legs... I mean who wouldn't... oh behave! When he is in daycare, he always greets me by running between my legs and when we are out on our adventures, and I call him back to me his first thing to do is to go between my legs and wait eagerly for his treat.

How to teach the middle command

1. Have some yummy treats in both hands
2. With one hand lure your dog behind your leg
3. With the other hand use the treat to lure him through, so he is standing between your legs
4. Reward him with a yummy treat when he is between your legs

5. Throw out a treat in front of you and say OK to release your dog

6. Repeat the above several times a day and after a few days and once you feel your dog has got the hang of it, you can start to introduce the command word i.e. middle.

7. Say the command middle just as you lure your dog between your legs and then praise with a yummy treat when they are in position.

The purpose of this exercise is to have a safe place for your dog to retreat too. It is ideal for recall work, but as discussed in this chapter, it has a number of other benefits. You can even start walking with your dog when in the middle position if you want to, this would be particularly good when trying to distract him from that running squirrel or flock of birds. Have him come in the middle and then turn him around away from the distraction.

As with any form of training, you need to practice in an area of low distraction and build up to higher levels of distractions and remember the golden rule practice makes perfect. Eventually, you want to take away the lure and have your dog perform the action by voice command only.

Now that we have covered the indoor lessons we can now progress to taking your walks outside, and in the next chapter, I am going to show you how you can have your dog walk nicely on a loose lead alongside you.

Chapter Twelve
Taking your walks outside

We have covered a lot so far, but now we are going to look at taking your training outdoors into the big open world, a place full of distractions... what could possibly go wrong?

The answer is plenty... that's of course if you don't follow the lessons I have been sharing with you.

Within this chapter, I am going to share with you my top secrets on how to get your dog to walk nicely alongside you on a loose lead.

We now need to bring the lessons we have been working on indoors to outdoors. These lessons are the 'look at me' which remember we use to get our dog focused on us to avoid them jumping towards other people or dogs or anything that might take their fancy really. We will be making use of the traffic light system, especially on street walks and near roads and we will, of course, be adapting the wobble game. Do not worry I don't expect you to act drunk outside, I don't want your neighbours all talking about you as you stumble past their window.

The lessons we have already covered are so important when teaching your dog to walk nicely on a loose lead and you will soon start to see the benefits as with some practice and a little bit of patience, I am confident that by the end of this chapter you will have a loose lead with your dog walking nicely alongside you.

First of all, we need to refer back to Chapter seven, starting your walk off on a calm. If you want the results, you need to have a calm dog from the word go. A hyped-up dog, desperate to be outdoors is not going to end well, and you will end up getting frustrated and not getting the results you expected when you started reading this amazing (can I say that?) book.

I would advise initially working on your dog's lead training in the front street and around the houses mostly because there are fewer distractions there than say down at the beach when there could potentially be hundreds of off-lead dogs running around.

I will say again, when it comes to training something new, you start in areas of low distraction, and you build them up gradually.

Once we step outside the front door and your dog is calm, then training starts immediately. Start as you mean to go on, ask your dog to sit whilst you lock your front door, remember nothing in life is free and if you keep getting him to work for his rewards, he will be keener to please, and you will get the results you want quicker.

Now we start with the traffic light system that we discussed in chapter nine. You have already got your dog to sit as you lock the front door, there is your amber, now let us move onto the green...'walk-on' as you walk on start to issue the close command that we discussed in chapter ten (the wobble game).

Go back to the basics and praise after only a couple of steps, to begin with, remembering, of course, to say the command 'close' before treating. This will really help to reinforce the training you have been doing indoors but don't forget outside in the big open world there are so many distractions we have to expect sometimes that things won't always go to plan therefore we need a back-up plan.

The turn command –

The turn command is what we use if your dog attempts to pull in front of you. If this happens, you need to STOP and with the use of a treat lure your dog to turn around and face the opposite direction. Remember we want him to do it voluntarily, we don't want to force him to turn. As you turn around the issue the command 'turn'. Once you are facing the opposite direction, continue to walk in that direction and if he pulls again repeat. This will help him to keep focus on you for direction and after time when he is walking nicely alongside you, then you can revert back to the close command.

An example of how this would look if your dog was pulling on the lead

1. Ask the dog to sit (amber)
2. Ask the dog to walk on (green)

3. Issue the close command and praise the dog for being alongside you
4. If the dog pulls STOP
5. With a treat, lure the dog around to face the opposite direction
6. When you are both facing the opposite direction, and your dog is alongside you, then you can issue the walk on command once more
7. If he pulls, STOP and repeat points 5 and 6

After a few attempts, you should find that you are able to get more and more steps without him pulling ahead but remember to make use of the close command and make use of this command frequently at the beginning. Only after time and practice will you start to increase the steps you take before issuing the close command before issuing the treat.

Within the bonus section of this book, you will find a link for a video tutorial regarding the turn command, so please make sure you give it a watch as if you are like me you will benefit from a visual as well.

I should point out that your neighbours may think you have lost the plot a little bit when you bring your training outside as you may find at the beginning stages you do not get very far forward, and you are constantly turning around... maybe they will think you are drunk after all. Allow extra times on your walk and do not worry if initially, you do not get very far, trust me you will be working your dog hard as he tries to understand what you want from him.

It won't be long before you are taking a number of steps before issuing the close command and before you know it 10 minutes could have gone by, and your dog is still walking calmly on a loose lead beside you. There are two things you need to do at this stage

1. Make sure you keep praising him every now and then to reinforce the close command.
2. Make sure you leave me a glowing report on Amazon and be sure to tell all of your friends how much you enjoyed training your dog the Pets2impress way.

So now we are at the stage where he is walking nicely alongside you, we can start to bring in the red part of the traffic light system, the stop command.

I personally would be using this command around roads, but I would also every now and then issue the stop command to keep your dog focused before you ask him to walk on.

You can start this training indoors to begin with, once you have this perfected then and only then should we look at increasing the level of distraction. The old saying is don't run before you can walk, and that certainly applies to lead training. Start gradually indoors to begin with and then move to the garden and then move to the back lane and then move to the streets.

You are now at a stage where you can refer back to chapter six, the look at me command. You would use this as you approach a dog or person or anything that may distract your dog. This prevents a lot of unwanted behaviours, but it also re-focuses the dog back on to you.

So, remember when taking your lead training outdoors to make sure your dog is calm before you begin, make use of the traffic light system, the wobble game and if necessary, use the turn command if he starts to pull ahead.

Now that we have addressed your dog's lead training, we can move on to your dog's outdoor recall training… I hope you ordered your whistle because you will need it in this next chapter.

Chapter Thirteen
Letting your dog off the lead for the first time

If you have never done this before, then trust me your heart will be in your mouth the first time you do it, but you have to have faith in yourself and your dog, and over time your confidence will continue to grow.

It is during this chapter that we will get to see the benefits of the 'name game' discussed in chapter four and the tail wagging game we discussed in chapter five.

We will also be bringing your whistle training outdoors.

I would advise that you begin by finding an area with low distraction, for example, don't go down to the beach where you risk having hundreds of other dogs and people. You want to try and find somewhere reasonably quiet as this will help keep your dog focused on you during the early stages of recall.

Whatever you do, do not forget your high-value treats and your whistle.

Once you have found a nice quiet area, now is the time to be brave and remove the lead. If you have never let your dog off the lead before and you are feeling a bit worried, you could try attaching a long line as discussed in chapter 2.

Long lines come in different lengths and in fact, we use them a lot when we take new daycare dogs out for the first time.

It is a way of allowing your dog the freedom to run, but it helps give you the confidence and reassurance that if you need him, you can grab a hold of the long line or put your foot on it.

Long lines are readily available, and you should easily be able to pick one up from your local pet shop or online.

Whether you decide to use the longline or you are brave enough to let him off his lead completely now is the important part and now we need to remember everything we have covered so far.

Allow your dog to go in front and then give your whistle a good blow, as soon as he turns to look at you, which he should if you have practised enough indoors with extra high-value treats now you need to revert back to the tail wagging game that we discussed in chapter five. What motivates your dog? What excites him? It's now time to use that.

The whistle will be great to get your dog's attention, but now we need to make sure we keep his attention and prevent him from getting distracted by something else. Jump up and down, slap your thighs, run in the opposite direction, say your dog's name in a high-pitched voice or make use of that special something that he loves such as his favourite toy or in some cases a feather. Personally, I do not care what you use as longs your dog loves what you have to offer.

I don't care what you have to do to get him to come to you just do it and don't worry about what others may think; the main thing is your dog is listening to you and coming back to you when you call him.

Praise him as he starts running towards you, reinforce this behaviour and when he gets to you quickly encourage him to do the middle command. When between your legs grab hold of his collar and praise him with that high-value treat.

One error a lot of owners make is they just call their dog back when it comes to home time. This is a major mistake made by so many owners because the dog soon learns that coming to you isn't actually as fun as he thought as all it means is playtime is over, time to go back home.

When I was a child my Mam used to take me to an outdoor water park, this has sadly now been demolished for many years now so I can't take my children, but I always remember it being the best place on earth. We used to go there a number of times each summer, and it probably wasn't that exciting when I look back, but as a child, it was so much fun. Me and my brother used to run wild, and we always had the most fun but then came those dreaded words... "Kids, 5 minutes then we are going". That would always result in me and my brother hiding as far away from our Mam as we could, don't worry it was fully enclosed we were not neglected and nor were we able to do everything we wanted.

The point is when those 5 minutes came, we ended up getting an extra 10 minutes as our Mam had to come and find us, so we felt a small bit of victory, that's until she found us and told us off. Ultimately, we still ended up being put back in the car, and we still ended up going back home, but the thrill of the chase made it all the more exciting, and that's something I see a lot with dog owners. They only call their dog back to them when it is home time, and because they clearly have never read this book, they don't follow the correct rules and as they reach down to go and grab the dog's collar to put the lead on the dog backs away and before you know it the owner and dog get into a game of chase, with the dog normally winning.

Over time the dog will have learnt that the owner calling them and then reaching for the collar can only mean one thing, playtime is over and so just like me and my brother did the dog rebels against the owner.

Imagine though if every time my Mam called us over, she gave us £5. I can guarantee I would be there in a flash, which kid wouldn't?

That is what we need to be doing with our dogs; we need to be calling them intermittently on their walk, and each time they come to you, reward them with that high-value treat and then send them off again to have some more fun.

Ultimately, yes there will come a time when we need to call our dog back because they do need to go on the lead, but that's fine, and by following these simple tips you won't get into a game of chase, you won't be late for work, you won't fall flat in the mud trying to catch him, and you won't have others laughing at you as you try to catch your dog.

If there is more than one person at home, you can also play the in between game. Think of it as a game of tennis with your dog being the ball... please note I am not suggesting you get a bat and bat your dog between you but instead stand so many metres apart and call your dog between you. Use the whistle, use your body language and see who can get the dog back to them the most. Very similar to the tail wagging game, see who can get the best recall from their dog. It's a fun game and a game your dog will want to get involved in.

You then start playing hide and seek with your dog by having one person hold on to the dog's collar whilst the other ones goes and hides behind a tree and then get the dog to come and find you. I loved playing hide and seek with Lady as she always used her nose to find me. As with the in-between game, this just reinforces to your dog how exciting it is being with you, and that's exactly what recall is, always making being with you a fun part of your walk.

Recall is one of the most important lessons you can ever teach your dog. It is the one lesson that could potentially save your dog's life, so make sure you take your time with the training and most importantly keep it fun.

Thankfully these days there are so many dog fields available for hire where you can take your dog to an enclosed field and work on their recall. The beauty of this is you know your dog can't go anywhere so if you are really reluctant to let your dog off the lead maybe think about trying a dog park to begin with to help with your confidence.

Don't be one of those owners that walks around on their phone constantly, ignoring the dog and allowing the dog to do whatever he wants, engage with the dog, make him want to keep focused on you. You need to really make use of your body language and remember when calling his name to keep it fun and positive.

Use the whistle to get his attention, body language to keep his attention, middle command, collar and then treat. Follow those rules, and you can't go wrong.

Over time build up the level of distraction, and you never know, eventually you might be able to let him off on the beach without the worry he is going to run to each and every dog he sees.

Now that we have the foundations of recall covered, I want to share with you how and why you should be making every walk into an adventure for both you and your dog.

Chapter Fourteen
Making every walk into an adventure.

Being out with your dog should be an enjoyable experience for both you and your dog, it shouldn't have to be a stressful event, and it certainly shouldn't be something you dread doing every day.

Throughout this book, I have shared with you a lot of my tips and secrets on how to get your dog to walk nicely alongside you and how to have the perfect recall but now is probably one of the most important lessons yet and that's keeping your dog's focus on you, so he is not easily distracted by everything else that is going on around him.

In October 2019, I introduced our brand-new adventures which is an additional service as part of our daycare. All dogs that attend daycare follow routine and structure, and they all go out for walks, they all enjoy some group and 1-1 training sessions, they all engage in some form of scent work, they get calms and cuddles, controlled play, top to tail examinations twice a day and they all go down for naps. We like to run our daycare as close to a nursery style setting as possible. The best thing is all dogs that attend get both mental and physical stimulation which sadly so many dogs lack on a day-to-day basis. There is a reason why our daycare dogs get overly excited when they get dropped off in a morning, and that's because they know when they are here, they are going to have lots of fun.

The adventures were the icing on the cake for the dogs, and all owners have the opportunity for their dogs to go out on an adventure when they are with us.

An adventure is not just a case of leading the dog up, taking them somewhere fun and then watching them run around, running up to everyone and everything they see, the adventures were designed to give them further opportunities to have both mental and physical stimulation, and that's just what they get.

I enjoy being in the outdoors, especially when I have a dog by my side. I remember when I lost my last dog, Lady and I found being outside was just not the same without her by my side, hence why it wasn't long before we welcomed Buddy into our lives. I was, of course, lucky in the fact I have a job where I get to spend my days working with dogs, and there is nothing that I love more than being out on adventures with them, watching them do what they love doing the most... having fun.

Being an outdoors person, I see a lot of owners struggling with their dogs outdoors, they seem to have no control as their dog is running around crazy and chasing every other dog they see, jumping up at people and completely ignoring the owner when they call them back.

If you don't make walks fun for your dog, trust me, they will find other ways to make them fun, and that doesn't always involve you.

Walking around with your hands in your pocket with your head down or spending the walk playing on your phone will result in one thing, and that is a dog that loses focus on you. As discussed in previous chapters, you need to make yourself fun at all times. The world is a big place filled with lots of fun distractions, and if you are not careful you will lose your dog's attention to those distractions, maybe you already have which is why you are reading this book. Let us hope that you follow the advice in this book and trust me if you do, you won't look back.

So how do we make our walks into an adventure?

The open-world is one big adventure, and wherever you go trust me, you can make your walk into a fun adventure for both you and your dog.

Natural Agility

I am lucky where I live as I live near the coast so there are plenty of different locations to go every day to walk my dog and every day brings a new adventure.

When I go out, I'm not looking for which people or dogs I need to avoid; instead, I am looking at what I can find to get my dog to jump on or jump over. If I come across a fallen down tree, I have Buddy jumping over it or balancing on it. When I go to the forest, I have Buddy weaving in and out of the trees. I have a leisure centre in walking distance from my house and outside is an area where people park their peddle bikes, to many that's what they will see a place for people to park their bikes, but to me, I see an opportunity to get Buddy engaged in some natural outdoor Hoopers. Down at the beach I have him jumping on the rocks, I will throw his ball into the water (he's a whippet so just to ankle depth otherwise its bye bye ball). Dog's love to engage in natural agility, especially when they realise, they are going to get something for doing so.

One client even said to me that now she can't pass any form of natural agility without her dog wanting to have a go and the reason for that is the dog has learnt from association that this brings good things.

Wherever you go, you will find something that you can use to get your dog engaged. In the bonus section of this book, you will find a link for a YouTube video which will give you an example of some of the types of natural agility we do with our daycare dogs.

Scent Work

Dogs love nothing more than to use their nose, but sadly not many dogs get ample opportunities to use their nose as they are forever getting dragged away from owners. Unlike humans who have 5-6 million scent receptors in our noses, dogs (depending on the breed) can have up to 100 million or more scent receptors in their nose.

Just as we use vision as our primary sense for understanding our environment, dogs use their noses. The way something smells gives dogs more information than the way something looks, feels, sounds or tastes.

Preventing your dog from experiencing the world through scent is like sending us outside in a blindfold. The chance to smell provides your dog with important information plus it's a great way to provide your dog with more mental stimulation.

The benefits of scent work include

- It's stimulating
- It burns off energy
- It helps to build confidence
- It will help keep your dog fulfilled and content
- It helps reduce anxiety
- It helps keep your dog more focused

Take the Lead for the Perfect Recall

By providing your dog with ample opportunities to use their nose, ultimately it will make life easier for you. This is why we always encourage dogs to sniff, and this is why when out on our adventures, we set up scent trails, we hide treats in the sand or underneath fallen leaves.

It doesn't take a lot to get your dog's nose engaged, but it is certainly something you should be doing on each and every walk.

Training Time

Walks are not just about going to the field or the beach and then standing as you throw your dog's ball to burn off the energy. Yes, some dogs love the ball, and there is nothing wrong with playing with your dog and his ball, but that's not enough to keep your dog focused on you.

Training time is such a great way to bond with your dog, not only will it reinforce the nothing in life is free we discussed at the very beginning of the book, but it will also help keep your dog focused on you. After reading this book, you will have plenty of new things to be working on with your dog.

Play Time

Dogs love playing, and it offers a great form of enrichment. Adventures should also include playtime but don't just rely on a ball to keep your dog focused on you or as a way to burn off energy. Playtime is an important aspect of your dog's adventure, and it is a great way to build on that strong bond you no doubt already have.

Constantly throwing your dog's ball as you stand on the field or the beach can be fun, but it can also add a lot of strain to your dog's joints. I was guilty of this with Lady when she was a puppy I thought it was the perfect way to burn off the bounds of energy she had, but I was wrong and only when I started to make her walks into adventures did I start to see the difference and benefits an adventure can offer to your dog.

Make every walk an adventure, and I can guarantee you will keep your dog's focus and attention purely on you and not what is going on around him. As I write this chapter earlier today, I took one of our daycare dogs out for her first adventure. She has only been coming to daycare for one week, but throughout the whole walk, she was 100% focused on me.

Not once did she attempt to run away or go and say hello to another dog and why? The answer is simple… I made myself fun and interesting, and that encouraged her to keep her focus on me. I didn't even need to use the long line I had in my adventure bag.

This is what some of our daycare clients think about the adventures we offer at Pets2impress

"My lovely Labrador, Chip is very high energy, full of mischief and always ready for fun! I thought he would enjoy a day of adventure daycare. Chip has been going to daycare almost every day for over three years and absolutely loves it, and he clearly had an amazing time on his adventure day too! The pictures and videos were fantastic, and you could see how engaged and happy he was to be getting that extra 1-1 attention, training and stimulation. The trainers are amazing, and it's so easy to feel secure in the knowledge that your dog is in the best hands. He came home after his adventure very content and very tired. He can't wait for his next one!" **Justine Hunter**

"The adventure days are an amazing daycare addition and perfect for my dog Missy as she loves being outdoors and have the 1-1 attention. It shows how much she is enjoying both the physical and mental stimulation side as she comes home a very tired girl, plus it is great to see the fun she has in the photos and videos. Our walks are also more enjoyable now as we have more fun looking for things we can use to do agility with (which Missy loves to do), also doing training sessions. I think it is helping to create a closer bond and confidence between us, and I am also seeing an improvement in her recall with me. Great service! Thank you" **Debbie Gibbon**

After reading this chapter, the only thing you need to ask yourself is how exciting are you making walks for your dog and what can you do on your next walk to make that walk into an adventure… trust me you won't regret it. If you make your walks into an adventure and introduce everything we discussed in this chapter, it will make a 1 hour walk seem like a 4 hour walk for your dog.

Chapter Fifteen
Retractable leads

I did mention in a previous chapter that I was not a fan of retractable leads which is why I have decided to dedicate a full chapter to them.

I totally understand why people get retractable leads, it's a way of giving your dog some freedom instead of letting them off-lead, however, you will never have a dog that walks nicely alongside you when you train them on a retractable lead.

Dogs are not stupid, whether they are on a short retractable lead or they have full stretch of the lead they are still aware of the fact that they are on a lead and therefore cannot understand why one minute you want them to walk alongside you and then the next they are able to pull in front of you.

If you want your dog to walk alongside you, bin the retractable lead and make use of a good old-fashioned collar and lead... now that you have perfected your dog's recall hopefully you will realise that you don't need a retractable lead anymore.

Apart from not being able to teach your dog to walk nicely alongside you, retractable leads are also, in my opinion, a very dangerous tool to use.

When I worked in practice, I will always remember a little dog that was brought in as an emergency as sadly he had just been ran over. The story behind the accident was the owner was walking him on his retractable lead alongside a busy main road, and he had full stretch of his lead. Normally he would just sniff the walls or the lampposts, but on this occasion, he saw another dog on the opposite side of the road. This dog did not like other dogs and so started to react. The owner got a shock by the situation, and accidentally let go of the lead. As the plastic handle of the retractable lead fell to the floor the noise of the bang as it hit frightened the dog, and the dog ran, but as he ran the plastic handle kept banging off the floor which continued to frighten him and therefore, he didn't stop running, that was until sadly a car hit him.

Thankfully, he made a full recovery and was incredibly lucky, and I think it's safe to say the owner never used the retractable lead again. During my time in practice and as a canine behaviourist, I have also lost count with how many leads have snapped or caused issues as dogs have tied themselves around the owner or around other people.

One owner I spoke to several years ago had her dog on an extendable lead, and he managed to tie himself around another dog. This caused distress to the other dog, and then that dog bit her dog, which resulted in a visit to the vets and that dog then as a result of that incident developed fear-based aggression towards other dogs.

I could write a full book on different incidents that owners have had with their dog whilst being on an extendable and from a safety point of view this is one of the main reasons, I do not recommend them.

From a training point of view, I just feel you are fighting a losing battle and ultimately making life more difficult for yourself, so although this was a very short chapter, I felt it was an important one and if you do anything after reading this chapter make sure you bin the retractable lead, follow the advice in this book and trust me you won't ever need to go back to one again. Hopefully, you have been lucky enough not to have encountered any accidents with your dog, but I have spoken to many that have, and it's just not worth it.

Chapter Sixteen
Your key to success

We have covered a lot of different lessons within this book, but if you want to see those results out on your walks, you need to begin by putting in the work. Only you can correct your dog's pulling on the lead, and only you can help your dog achieve a perfect recall.

You need to begin by ensuring you have the correct pieces of equipment as detailed in Chapter two (hopefully avoiding a retractable lead following on from the last chapter). You then need to start as you mean to go on and start implementing the nothing in life is free into every aspect of your dog's life. Make them work for everything, reinforce the good and ignore the bad and remember those golden rules when ignoring the unwanted behaviours 1. Do not look 2. Do not touch and 3. Do not speak.

Have a look at how you can add some structure to your dog's day-to-day life with the use of a routine. Make sure everyone in the family gets involved, training should not just fall down to one person.

For your dog's lead training, we have discussed a number of different lessons this includes the 'look at me' command which you will use to refocus your dog's attention back on to you and to prevent your dog from lunging, jumping up or just acting problematically around other distractions. Make sure you follow the step by step guide on how to have a perfect 'look at me' command.

Make sure you practice with the Traffic light system and the wobble game. It will take time to teach your dog these new commands so try not to rush them. Remember with any form of training to practice indoors to begin with, and only when your dog is confidently performing the commands should you look at increasing the level of distraction.

When you are ready to take your training outdoors, make sure you start your walks off on a calm and remember to reinforce that calm behaviour at all times. A dog bouncing up and down like a kangaroo is not going to be easy to train outdoors, so be sure to follow the advice in this book to help calm him down.

When it comes to taking the lead training outdoors, remember everything you have been working on.

- Look at me
- Turn
- Sit
- Go
- Stop
- Turn

Don't let your hard work go down the drain, take your time, be patient and consistent at all times.

Recall training may be the one part that you are less confident doing but trust me by following my training tips within this book, you can't go wrong. Remember the hard work you put in with the 'name game' and the 'tail wagging game'. Remember to make use of your whistle, your body language and the 'middle' command.

Most importantly make sure you make every walk into an adventure and always have fun. If you have fun, your dog will want to join in on that fun with you.

No longer should taking your dog for a walk be a stressful part of the day, hopefully after reading this book and implementing my top tips you can start to enjoy your walks again and build on that everlasting bond you already have with your dog.

The final thing I want to share with you before you go and make a start with your dog's training is to keep a record of your dog's progress. As humans, we always tend to focus more on the negatives, but by having a training log, you can look back and see just how well your dog is progressing. If you focus more on the positives, trust me, the negatives will start to slowly disappear.

Bonuses

I hope you have enjoyed reading this book, and I hope it has left you feeling motivated and ready to tackle this common issue. Just remember that this book is only valuable if you take action.

I do appreciate that there is only so much you can take away from a book which is why I have decided to share some free gifts with you.

My first gift to you is a free copy of the Pets2impress Training guide. This will help with your dog's basic training requirements.

Visit the link below to grab your copy
https://mailchi.mp/17e466208370/free-training-guide

My second gift to you is a PDF version of recycle the recycling which will give you some ideas for some home-made brain games to use with your dog.

Visit the link below to grab your copy
https://mailchi.mp/c877fefbe914/recycletherecycling

My third gift to you is a PDF version of some home-made cake recipes for your dog for you to try and use during your dog's training.

Visit the link below to grab your copy
https://mailchi.mp/79f391e0fb80/cakerecipes

My fourth gift to you is free access to some tutorial videos which will hopefully help with your dog's training.

Visit the link below to watch these tutorial videos
https://mailchi.mp/4d0da71e19b7/lead-and-recall-tutorial-videos

And my fifth gift to you is some videos to show you some of our day-care dogs on their adventure to give you some ideas on how to make your dog's walk into an adventure.

Visit the links below to watch the videos

https://youtu.be/s79d7i2_Hss	https://youtu.be/7WhP2_pz5RE
https://youtu.be/UPZO7uFKjQw	https://youtu.be/fiDOxDty5zw

As a thank you for these gifts, please feel free to leave a glowing review on Amazon for me.

About the Author

Tim Jackson started his career working with animals as a veterinary auxiliary nurse. He trained and qualified as a veterinary nurse in 2007 at Myerscough College. He was promoted to Head veterinary nurse and spent a number of years helping animals and their owners.

In 2008, Tim launched Pets2impress, a company that took the region by storm. What began as a pet sitting service soon expanded to offer a variety of services.

In 2013, Tim took the decision to leave his position as Head Veterinary nurse to expand Pets2impress.

Tim has completed multiple animal behaviour courses, including the Think Dog Certificates and a Diploma in Animal Behaviour. He passed each of these with a distinction and the knowledge he gained from these, combined with his extensive nursing experience, allowed him to offer one-on-one training sessions for all problem behaviours utilising only positive, reward-based training programmes.

This is a fun and stress-free method of training, which is easy to learn and rapidly achieves fantastic results. In its most basic form, it is a method of communication that is very clear for the dog. Examples of problem behaviours which Tim is able to assist with include separation anxiety, lack of basic training, dog-on-dog aggression and other anxiety-related issues, however, no problem is too small or too big for Tim.

In 2015, Tim opened a state-of-the-art daycare facility, offering a safe and stimulating environment for dogs whilst their owners' are out at work. His experience as a qualified veterinary nurse, dog trainer and canine behaviourist gave him a comprehensive understanding that all dogs have different physical and emotional needs, allowing daycare sessions to be tailor-made to suit each individual.

Tim runs his daycare as close to a nursery setting as possible and therefore follows a daily schedule as closely as possible. This is extremely beneficial to the dogs in his care as it has been well documented that dogs thrive off predictability, and it has positive effects on both their behaviour and mental wellbeing.

A typical day at the daycare centre includes free play, walks outside for a change of scenery, training-time, and quiet time as rest is extremely important to prevent overstimulation, which can have a negative impact on both behaviour and physical condition. In October 2019, Tim launched an additional package to the daycare service, the doggy 'adventure' daycare to offer dog's further opportunity to receive physical and mental stimulation on a 1-1 basis as well as receive the other benefits daycare has to offer. In June 2020, Tim launched two additional packages to the daycare service, The Scent Space and School Trips as with the adventure daycares these were designed to allow dogs further opportunity to receive physical and mental stimulation. In September 2020 Tim launched his brand-new unique daycare membership club which is filled with so many benefits for owners and their dogs.

Tim is well known for his sense of humour and love and dedication to the welfare of all animals. Tim has owned several animals over the years including a rescue tarantula (which he was absolutely terrified of), an iguana, bearded dragons, cats, hamsters, rats, mice, fish and dogs.

Tim's mission in life is to help owners who struggle with their dog to prevent dogs from ending up in shelter.

When not working Tim can be seen swapping Doggy daycare for Daddy daycare. Tim loves nothing more than spending time with his three adorable children. He can also be found out walking his dog Buddy and every now and then enjoys a nice pint at the local pub.

To find out more about Tim and Pets2impress please visit the Pets2impress website www.pets2impress.com

Other Books by the Author

Available to purchase from www.pets2impress.com and Amazon

Dog Training Book

Help! My dog is a devil with other dogs

Help! My dog doesn't like being left alone

Acknowledgements

As this is my third book, there are so many people I would like to thank, so many people that have supported me over the years and pushed me to always try harder. I definitely forgot to say thanks to certain people in my last two books, oops... I'll try harder in this book.

My first thanks must go to my adorable dogs that I have had over the years, it is thanks to them that I found my love for dog training and dog behaviour. Gone but never forgotten I would like to dedicate this book to my first dog Pip, Lady, Rosie and my two current dogs, Buddy and Bea.

To my family and friends, who are always there when I need them. I wouldn't be the person I am today without you.

Special thanks to my wife, Rebecca, and my three adorable children, Sienna, Harvey and Darcey. They give me a purpose to continue working hard.

Special thanks to my good friend Tim Strange who has been there for me whenever I have needed him.

Special thanks to my good friend Annouska Muzyczuk who have always stuck by me through thick and thin.

To my mentor, Dominic Hodgson, for his guidance and support and for continuing to push me forward.

To my good friend, Katie Gee, from Dogwood Adventure Play, for recommending me to Dominic Hodgson and for your support over the years. Working together at Dogs Trust, she tolerated a lot of shit from me as we travelled around the country.

To my good friend, Shannon, who is always a phone call away should I ever need to talk or in some cases moan. One of the few people that can really make me belly laugh. An extra thank you to Shannon for providing me with a brilliant cover for this book, she really caught my best side.

Shannon is an amazing photographer. Check out some of her other projects via her Facebook page, 'Shannon Nixon Photography'.

To my good friend, Georgie, who is my training partner and who encourages me to keep going even when I really do not want to.

To my personal trainer and friend, Steve, who always encourages me to push forward.

To my good friend, Suresh, who has always encouraged and guided me and has always helped me out when I needed him.

To the staff at Pets2impress, Shannon, Lauren, Abby, Abbey, Terri and Karen 1. For putting up with me all of these years and laughing at my not so funny jokes and 2. For your support, enthusiasm and shared love you have for the dogs in our care. I couldn't do the job I do without my amazing team.

To my Pets2impress clients, who have been loyal to Pets2impress all these years. I would not be where I am today without your support, recommendations and dedication.

To the veterinary staff, who I used to work with for their support and recommendations over the years. They certainly had to put up with a lot from me, from singing constantly to winding each of them up on a daily basis. I certainly miss working with them every day.

My final thanks must go to you. Thank you for choosing this book and spending the time to read it. I hope you found it useful and I hope you start to action the points made in this book. My mission is to try and prevent as many dogs ending up in shelter if possible, and if this book helps others, then I can sleep well at night. I ask if you found this book useful that you leave a review on Amazon... I will accept no less than a 5-star rating.

Tim Jackson, RVNBCCSDip.Fda

Printed in Great Britain
by Amazon